The
Acceptance
and
Commitment
Therapy
(ACT) Diary

**A guide and companion for moving
toward the things that matter in your life**

2023

Dr Nic Hooper and Dr Freddy Jackson Brown

The Acceptance and Commitment Therapy (ACT) Diary 2023

Published by:
Pavilion Publishing and Media Ltd
Blue Sky Offices
Cecil Pashley Way
Shoreham by Sea
West Sussex
BN43 5FF
Tel: 01273 434 943
Fax: 01273 227 308
Email: info@pavpub.com

Published 2022

ISBN: 9781803882154

Pavilion Publishing and Media is a leading publisher of books, training materials and digital content in mental health, social care and allied fields. Pavilion and its imprints offer must-have knowledge and innovative learning solutions underpinned by sound research and professional values.

Cover design: Phil Morash, Pavilion Publishing and Media Ltd.
Page layout and typesetting: Phil Morash, Pavilion Publishing and Media Ltd.
Printing: Ashford Press

*"Every accomplishment starts
with the decision to try."*

John F. Kennedy

Contents

2023 Year Planner

	January	February	March	April	May	June
Sun	1					
Mon	2				1	
Tue	3				2	
Wed	4	1	1		3	
Thu	5	2	2		4	1
Fri	6	3	3		5	2
Sat	7	4	4	1	6	3
Sun	8	5	5	2	7	4
Mon	9	6	6	3	8	5
Tue	10	7	7	4	9	6
Wed	11	8	8	5	10	7
Thu	12	9	9	6	11	8
Fri	13	10	10	7	12	9
Sat	14	11	11	8	13	10
Sun	15	12	12	9	14	11
Mon	16	13	13	10	15	12
Tue	17	14	14	11	16	13
Wed	18	15	15	12	17	14
Thu	19	16	16	13	18	15
Fri	20	17	17	14	19	16
Sat	21	18	18	15	20	17
Sun	22	19	19	16	21	18
Mon	23	20	20	17	22	19
Tue	24	21	21	18	23	20
Wed	25	22	22	19	24	21
Thu	26	23	23	20	25	22
Fri	27	24	24	21	26	23
Sat	28	25	25	22	27	24
Sun	29	26	26	23	28	25
Mon	30	27	27	24	29	26
Tue	31	28	28	25	30	27
Wed			29	26	31	28
Thu			30	27		29
Fri			31	28		30
Sat				29		
Sun				30		
Mon						

2023 Year Planner

	July	August	September	October	November	December
Sun				1		
Mon				2		
Tue		1		3		
Wed		2		4	1	
Thu		3		5	2	
Fri		4	1	6	3	1
Sat	1	5	2	7	4	2
Sun	2	6	3	8	5	3
Mon	3	7	4	9	6	4
Tue	4	8	5	10	7	5
Wed	5	9	6	11	8	6
Thu	6	10	7	12	9	7
Fri	7	11	8	13	10	8
Sat	8	12	9	14	11	9
Sun	9	13	10	15	12	10
Mon	10	14	11	16	13	11
Tue	11	15	12	17	14	12
Wed	12	16	13	18	15	13
Thu	13	17	14	19	16	14
Fri	14	18	15	20	17	15
Sat	15	19	16	21	18	16
Sun	16	20	17	22	19	17
Mon	17	21	18	23	20	18
Tue	18	22	19	24	21	19
Wed	19	23	20	25	22	20
Thu	20	24	21	26	23	21
Fri	21	25	22	27	24	22
Sat	22	26	23	28	25	23
Sun	23	27	24	29	26	24
Mon	24	28	25	30	27	25
Tue	25	29	26	31	28	26
Wed	26	30	27		29	27
Thu	27	31	28		30	28
Fri	28		29			29
Sat	29		30			30
Sun	30					31
Mon	31					

Personal Information

Name:

Address:

Home Phone Number:

Mobile Phone Number:

Email:

Office Phone Number:

Work Address:

If you find this diary please contact:

Welcome to the Acceptance and Commitment Therapy (ACT) Diary 2023.

Get yourself a cup of tea or coffee, sit down in a comfortable chair, and let's make a start.

Introduction

The Acceptance and Commitment Therapy (ACT) Diary 2023 is designed to help you move toward the things that are important to you over the coming year. If this is the second, third, fourth, fifth or even sixth time that you are using our diary then you'll know what to expect. We do hope that focusing on your values will continue to positively impact your wellbeing.

As psychologists and fellow human beings who are committed to creating innovative and practical ways to foster wellbeing, we've put together this diary to help you make meaningful changes in your life. "We" is Dr Nic Hooper and Dr Freddy Jackson Brown. In fact, given that we'll be spending so much time together, it may be useful to see us as a couple of friends, speaking from the heart to help you move in positive directions. If you are interested, you can find out more about each of us at the back of this diary.

We know from our experience of making meaningful changes (and supporting many others to do so) that there's a big gap between knowing what we should be doing and actually *doing* it. And an even bigger gap between doing something once and maintaining our progress. We've designed this diary to help you bridge these gaps.

The diary is based on 'Acceptance and Commitment Therapy' or 'ACT' ('ACT' is usually said as one word), which is an evidence-based approach to human suffering that aims to increase what's called *psychological flexibility*. In non-jargon terms, this means connecting fully with all of our experiences, including difficult thoughts and feelings, whilst doing things that are personally meaningful.

"But what does ACT actually involve?", we hear you ask. Well, ACT aims to improve wellbeing by using six simple but fundamental skills that build our psychological flexibility. Let's introduce you to two of them:

Values:
In some ways, the whole point of ACT is to help people live in a way that's consistent with their personal values. In order to do that, we need to be clear about what our values are, or what's important to us.

Committed Action:
Values remain only nice ideas unless we express them in our behaviours. Values-based actions bring our values to life.

Introduction

Essentially, the more we live in line with what matters to us the better our psychological health will be. However, life isn't that simple. Often, our understandable but unwanted thoughts, feelings, worries and doubts can be barriers to valued action. Our minds, in trying to keep us safe, sometimes predict the worst. An example of this might be as follows:

> *Imagine you were just about to ask someone out on a date in the pursuit of a romantic relationship. What thoughts and feelings would be happening for you? If it were us, we'd have feelings of quite severe anxiety and our minds would probably feed us thoughts like "They might not be interested in me, so I'll look very silly if I ask them out."*

If we follow the advice of our doubting minds, then we might feel relief in the short-term; however, we run the risk of missing out in the longer term because we won't be moving towards our values. Instead, it can be useful to relate to our thoughts and feelings more flexibly, simply acknowledging that they are there whilst continuing to move towards what matters. ACT offers four more skills to help us with this:

Willingness:
We humans often try our utmost to avoid negative and uncomfortable thoughts and feelings. However, avoidance of our internal experiences has the habit of pulling us away from doing what matters. If we can learn to make room for them and take them along for the ride, then we'll be freer to engage in meaningful action.

Defusion:
We humans tend to be very attached to our own thoughts, seeing them as advice that we should comply with. However, if we can see them for what they are (just thoughts), create some healthy psychological distance from them, and hold them lightly, then we'll better be able to do the things that are important to us.

Contact With The Present Moment:
We humans spend 50% of our time ruminating about the past or worrying about the future. That's quite something. For example, divide your current age by half. The figure you came up with is the number of years you've likely not been living in the here-and-now. By contacting the present moment, we become better at appreciating the beauty and opportunity that surrounds us right now.

Observer Self:
We humans build stories about who we are that can serve to restrict us. But if we can instead observe our self-stories, and hold them lightly, then we'll be less imprisoned by them.

Introduction

The six parts of the ACT model are sometimes tied together in a beautifully simple diagram called *The Triflex*, which is shown opposite. The Triflex gives us three instructions for how to flourish in this game of life:

Open Up:
Defusion and *Willingness* involve spotting and making room for our uncomfortable thoughts and feelings.

Be Present:
Contact With The Present Moment and the *Observer Self* involve making contact with our experiences in the here-and-now.

Do What Matters:
Values and *Committed Action* involve figuring out what's important and moving towards it.

When we're not present, not open and not doing what matters to us, everyday life can feel less meaningful and more of a chore. We've all been there and know what this is like. And conversely, when we're present, open and doing what matters, we tend to feel more fulfilled and in tune with life and the people around us.

With these things in mind, your *ACT Diary* will help you to become connected to your moment-by-moment experiences (*Be Present*), and to embrace your unwanted thoughts and feelings (*Open Up*), so that you can move towards your values (*Do What Matters*).

The ACT Triflex

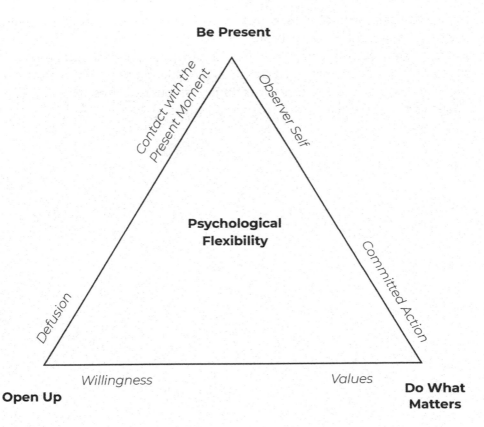

Be Present

Contact with the Present Moment

Observer Self

Defusion

Psychological Flexibility

Committed Action

Open Up

Willingness

Values

Do What Matters

© Russ Harris, 2009

How to Use Your ACT Diary

This diary is very easy to understand and use. To get the most from it, all you have to do is read and engage with our exercises and ideas, bring openness and curiosity to the process, and commit to making some changes that are in line with what's important to you.

To give yourself the best chance at developing and maintaining these skills, and embedding them into your daily life so that they can keep helping you for years into the future, you'll need to give your self-care and personal development the importance it deserves by making time each week to use the diary. You can use this time to engage with our exercises, to record your values and goals, and to reflect on your progress.

Space for general reflection

Throughout this diary we'll occasionally give you a page or two for general reflection. What you write here is up to you. You might want to think about how you're feeling, and what is contributing to you feeling that way. As you get further into the diary and the year, you could reflect on whether ACT, and a focus on values and goals in particular, is making a difference in your life.

We'll start each space for general reflection with the following broad pointers: "Use this space to record the ups and downs of the past few weeks. You may also want to write down what you have learned about yourself and the nature of life." These are based on what we ourselves use the section for, but they may not reflect what suits you best or what you choose to use it for.

You can start right away, on the following pages. Remember that there are no right and wrong answers. It's up to you to decide what to write – what you think might be valuable for you to set down now, and what might be potentially helpful to look back on from further along your journey.

Space for general reflection

Use this space to record the ups and downs of the past few weeks. You may also want to write down what you have learned about yourself and the nature of life.

Space for general reflection

Week 1

Welcome to Week 1.

Let's get going with an activity based on a very simple question:
What do you want?

Use the space on this page and opposite to list some of the things you'd like to achieve in the next few months. You could even think of these as your New Year's resolutions. At this point, don't worry about how big, small, possible or difficult these goals might be. Just list what pops into your head.

Once you have your list, choose a small goal, write it at the bottom of this page, and try to complete it over the next week. If you succeed, tick the box!

You can also write your goal in the summary box provided at the beginning of each weekly view (see next page for an example). This will help you keep in mind the things that you are striving to move towards and achieve.

🎯 Goal

Week 1

December 2022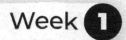

 Summary goal for the week

26  Monday

27  Tuesday

28  Wednesday

29 ACT  Thursday

30 ACT  Friday

31 ACT  Saturday

1 ACT Sunday

> *"Every moment
> is a fresh beginning."*
> *T.S. Eliot*

Week 2

Welcome to Week 2.

How did you get on? Did you complete the goal from Week 1?
Please take a moment to reflect on your experience of this. For example,
which goal did you choose to complete, why did you choose that goal, how
did you feel if you completed the goal, and if you didn't complete the goal
then what got in the way?

An Introduction to Values

Values are about how you want to behave, moment-by-moment, during your life. In some ways, they describe the sort of person you want to be. For example, if the value of *'caring'* is important to you then what can you do that reflects this value? How can you behave towards yourself, others and the environment in a caring way? People that live more in line with their values tend to be psychologically healthier. The thing most people say after we say those words is *'I don't even know what my values are'*. That is one thing this diary will help you with, as it is jam-packed with different ways of tuning into values.

We're going to start with a really simple exercise. We want you to imagine that you've won the lottery and below we'd like you to detail, in the left hand column, how you might spend your winnings. Leave the right-hand column blank for now. As an additional activity, please choose another goal from your Week 1 list, write it at the bottom of this page and try to complete it before we next speak.

 Goal

Summary goal for the week

 **2** **Monday**

 **3** **Tuesday**

 **4** **Wednesday**

January 2023

5 ACT  Thursday

6 ACT  Friday

7 ACT  Saturday   **8** ACT Sunday

> *"Lasting change is a series of compromises. And compromise is all right, as long your values don't change."*
>
> *Jane Goodall*

Week 3

Welcome to Week 3.

We asked you to do two things last week. Firstly, we asked you to complete another goal from the first list that you made in this diary. Did you manage to do it? As with Week 1, take a moment to reflect on your experience of trying (and maybe succeeding?) to do something important to you.

The other thing we asked you to do was to think about how you might spend your lottery winnings. We'd now like you to flick back to Week 2 and try to pin-point the possible values that are underneath your lottery spending (please write some of those values in the right hand column of that exercise). That is, once you get past the big houses and the fast cars, answers to the lottery question tend to reveal some important things in our lives. For example, *'self-care'*, *'travel'* or *'learning'* might be values underneath the words *'have lots of holidays'*. We'd now like you to write down a small goal that is in line with one of the values that the lottery question revealed, and try to complete it over the next week.

 Goal

Value Domains

From completing the lottery question you may begin to see that values exist in different domains of our life. These domains may or may not be important. Consequently, we'd like you to complete the exercise below in order to determine which areas are important to you and how much you neglect them. In column 2 please rate the overall importance of the domain to you on a scale of 1-10. In column 3 please rate how much behavioural attention you tend to give to that domain, in other words the extent to which you put it into action. Finally, please subtract the smaller number from the larger to create a *'concern'* score for each domain in column 4. The higher the number, the larger the discrepancy between what is important to you and how much you are acting in line with it.

	Importance (1-10)	Action (1-10)	Concern (1-10)
Friends and Social Relationships			
Work and Career			
Family Relationships			
Education and Learning			
Intimate Relationships			
Self-development and Growth			
Recreation and Leisure			
Spirituality			
Community and Citizenship			
Health and Physical Wellbeing			

January 2023

 Summary goal for the week

---

9  Monday

---

10 Tuesday

---

11  Wednesday

January 2023

12 ACT  **Thursday**

13 ACT  Friday

14 ACT  Saturday

15 ACT Sunday

> *"Try not to become a man of success but rather try to become a man of value."*
>
> **Albert Einstein**

Week 4

Welcome to Week 4.

Did you manage to complete the goal related to the lottery task? If so, what did you think and/or feel before, during and after you had completed the goal? If you did not complete the goal, what barriers (internal or external) stopped you?

Now look back to the domains exercise. Did you learn anything important? Which domain are you neglecting the most? In the space below we'd like you to record a goal that relates to the domain with the highest *'concern'* score and try to complete it over the next week.

 Goal

SMART Goals

Each week thus far we have asked you to complete a goal. However, we have done this without giving you any information about the best way to set goals in the first place (which is pretty naughty of us!). When you set goals for yourself, try to make them SMART (Specific, Measurable, Achievable, Relevant and Timely).

Specific: This is about being as precise as possible with regards to what you want to achieve. The more specific your description, the easier it is to know if you achieved it.

Measurable: This is about setting goals you can measure so that you know when you have achieved them.

Achievable: Is your goal really achievable? Setting goals that are unrealistic or a long way in the future makes life difficult. If you have a large goal, then it's better to break it down into smaller steps.

Relevant: This is about checking that the goal really reflects your underlying values. It is quite common to set goals that we think we *'should'* do, but deep down we may not really care about them.

Timely: This is about being clear when you will complete your goal. It is important to be precise about this.

Example of a SMART goal:

S	My goal is to lose weight (specific).
M	I will aim for 2 kg and I will exercise 3 times a week (measurable).
A	2kg is attainable based on my experience (achievable).
R	This is important to me because I value being healthy (relevant).
T	I will complete this goal within 2 months (timely).

January 2023

Week 4

 Summary goal for the week

 16 ACT **Monday**

 **17** ACT **Tuesday**

 **18** ACT **Wednesday**

January 2023

Week 4

19 ACT  Thursday

20 ACT  Friday

21 ACT  Saturday

22 ACT  Sunday

> "A goal without a plan is just a wish."
>
> *Antoine de Saint-Exupéry*

Week 5

Welcome to Week 5.

Did you manage to complete the goal related to the *'concern'* domain? If so, what did you think and/or feel before, during and after you had completed the goal? If not, what barriers (internal or external) stopped you? And did you make the goal SMART? If so, then great! If not, then remember to be as precise as possible when setting your goals.

Note: At the back of this diary you'll find a 'Goal Bank' where you can save any goals you don't manage to complete. Then you'll be able to return to those goals at some point in the future.

Ok, thus far you have had a gentle introduction to the concepts of goals and values but now we are going to start digging a little more! On the next page is a list of common values. We'd like you to cross out boxes until you have the three most important left (do this with a pencil so that you can use the values list as a reference point throughout the year). Then in the space below we'd like you to write down a goal that would bring one of those three values to life over the next week.

 Goal

Identifying Values

Having a life filled with novelty and change	Teaching others	Being at one with God	Being wealthy	Showing respect to parents and elders	Helping others
Maintaining the safety and security of my loved ones	Meeting my obligations	Being physically fit	Eating healthy food	Acting consistently with my religious beliefs	Being loyal to friends and family
Having a life filled with adventure	Being admired by many people	Making sure to repay favours and not be indebted to people	Having an exciting life	Being curious, discovering new things	Being safe from danger
Figuring things out, solving problems	Being self disciplined and resisting temptation	Engaging in sporting activities	Showing respect for tradition	Connecting with nature	Creating beauty (in any domain)
Building and repairing things	Promoting justice and caring for the weak	Being sexually desirable	Caring for others	Having a sense of accomplish-ment and making a lasting contribution	Striving to be a better person
Being competent and effective	Having influence over people	Accepting others as they are	Being honest	Having relationships involving love and affection	Enjoying music, art or drama
Researching things	Engaging in clearly defined work	Working with my hands	Being in charge	Being ambitious and hardworking	Acting with courage
Designing things	Competing with others	Being self sufficient	Being creative	Organising things	Gaining wisdom

January 2023

 Summary goal for the week

 23 **Monday**

 24 **Tuesday**

 25 **Wednesday**

January 2023

Week **5**

26 ACT  Thursday

27 ACT  Friday

28 ACT Saturday

29 ACT Sunday

66 "The true perfection of man lies
not in what man has, but in what man is."

Oscar Wilde

Space for general reflection

Use this space to record the ups and downs of the past few weeks. You may also want to write down what you have learned about yourself and the nature of life.

Space for general reflection

Week 6

Welcome to Week 6.

How did you get on? Did you manage to complete a goal related to the values list exercise from Week 5? If so, what did you think and/or feel before, during and after you had completed the goal? If you did not complete the goal, what barriers (internal or external) stopped you?

Sometimes the exercise from Week 5 by itself isn't enough to give people a sense of which values are important to them. Consequently, on the next page there is another values sorting exercise that we'd like you to complete. As with Week 5, we'd like you to cross out boxes until you have just three left (do this in pencil so you can use the values list as a reference point throughout the year). Then in the space below we'd like you to write down a goal that would bring one of those three values to life over the next week.

 Goal

Refining Values

Acceptance	Fairness	Order
Adventure	Fitness	Open-mindedness
Assertiveness	Flexibility	Patience
Authenticity	Friendliness	Persistence
Beauty	Forgiveness	Respect
Caring	Fun	Responsibility
Challenge	Generosity	Romance
Compassion	Gratitude	Self-care
Connection	Honesty	Self-development
Contribution	Humour	Sensuality
Courage	Humility	Spirituality
Creativity	Independence	Supportiveness
Curiosity	Intimacy	Trust
Encouragement	Justice	Write your own
Equality	Kindness	Write your own
Excitement	Love	Write your own

Summary goal for the week

 30 ACT Monday

 31 ACT Tuesday

 **1 ACT Wednesday**

2 ACT  **Thursday**

3 ACT  **Friday**

4 ACT  **Saturday**

5 ACT  **Sunday**

"If you can do what you do best and be happy, you're further along in life than most people."

Leonardo DiCaprio

Week 7

Welcome to Week 7.

How did you get on? Did you manage to complete a goal related to the values list exercise from Week 6? If so, what did you think and/or feel before, during and after you had completed the goal? If you did not complete the goal, what barriers (internal or external) stopped you?

_____

_____

_____

_____

_____

_____

_____

_____

_____

_____

Up to this point we have asked you to think about value domains and the different values that might be important to you. However, the interesting thing about values is that they can change depending on the domain. Consequently, in the coming weeks we are going to delve a little deeper again. Specifically, across each value domain we are going to ask you to write down (and complete) both a small and a bold goal. As a reminder, the value domains we identified in Week 5 were:

- Domain 1: Friends and Social Relationships
- Domain 2: Work and Career
- Domain 3: Family Relationships
- Domain 4: Education and Learning
- Domain 5: Intimate Relationships
- Domain 6: Self-development and Growth
- Domain 7: Recreation and Leisure
- Domain 8: Spirituality
- Domain 9: Community and Citizenship
- Domain 10: Health and Physical Wellbeing

February 2023

Domain 1: Friends and Social Relationships

From the values lists in Week 5 and Week 6, which value would you like to bring to life in the domain of *friends and social relationships*?

Please write a very small commitment, which aligns with this value, and is in this domain, to be completed over the next week.

 Goal

Now please write a bold commitment, which aligns with this value, and is in this domain, to be completed over the next two weeks.

 Goal

Please make a note of the barriers (both internal and external) that you think might stop you from completing these goals.

Summary goal for the week

---

6 Monday

---

7 ACT Tuesday

---

8  Wednesday

February 2023

 **9** ACT Thursday

 **10** ACT Friday

 **11** ACT Saturday

 **12** ACT Sunday

"My humanity is bound up in yours, for we can only be human together."

Desmond Tutu

Week 8

Welcome to Week 8.

How did you get on? Did you complete the small goal from the *friends and social relationships* domain? Please take a moment to reflect on your experience. For example, which goal did you choose to complete, why did you choose this goal, how did you feel if you completed the goal, and if you didn't manage to complete the goal then what got in the way?

If you haven't already done so then in the next week please try to complete the bold goal from the *friends and social relationships* domain. If you have already completed both the small and bold goals from Week 7 (or if it isn't appropriate to complete the bold goal this week), use the space below to write a couple more goals for this domain to complete over the next week.

 Goal

 Goal

Managing our Thoughts and Feelings

You will notice that we keep asking you to think about barriers. The reason for this is because people often let their own thoughts and feelings (internal barriers) stop them from doing things that are important. The more we understand these barriers, the more we are able to notice and overcome them. For example, once we are aware of how our thoughts and feelings are interfering with us doing the things that matter, then we can use some of ACT's core processes to manage them. These processes, which we introduced on pages 12-13 and which we will explore further in the coming weeks, are:

Willingness: We humans try our utmost to avoid negative and uncomfortable thoughts and feelings. However, if we can learn to take them along for the ride, then we will be freer to engage in action.

Defusion: We humans tend to be very attached to our own thoughts. However, if we can distance ourselves from them, and hold them lightly, then we will better be able to do the things that are important to us.

Contact with the present moment: We humans can spend a lot of time ruminating about the past or worrying about the future. However, by contacting the present moment we will be able to appreciate the beauty and opportunity that surrounds us in the now.

Observing self: We humans build stories about who we are that can serve to restrict us. However, if we can instead observe our stories, then we will be less imprisoned by them.

February 2023

 Summary goal for the week

13 Monday

14 Tuesday

15  Wednesday

February 2023

16 ACT  Thursday

17 ACT  Friday

18 ACT  Saturday

19 ACT Sunday

> "Small emotions are the great captains of our lives, and we obey without knowing it."
>
> *Vincent van Gogh*

Week 9

Welcome to Week 9.

How did you get on? Did you complete the bold goal (or an alternative goal) from the *friends and social relationships* domain? Please take a moment to reflect on your experience. For example, which goal did you choose to complete, why did you choose this goal, how did you feel if you completed the goal, and if you didn't manage to complete the goal then what got in the way?

Domain 2: Work and Career

From the values lists in Week 5 and Week 6, which value would you like to bring to life in the domain of *work and career*?

Please write a very small commitment, which aligns with this value, and is in this domain, to be completed over the next week.

 Goal

Now please write a bold commitment, which aligns with this value, and is in this domain, to be completed over the next two weeks.

 Goal

Please make a note of the barriers (both internal and external) that you think might stop you from completing these goals.

February 2023

 Summary goal for the week

---

20 **Monday**

---

21 **Tuesday**

---

22 **Wednesday**

23 ACT  **Thursday**

24 ACT  **Friday**

25 ACT  **Saturday**

26 ACT **Sunday**

*"Choose a job you love,
and you will never have to work
a day in your life."*

Confucius

Space for general reflection

Use this space to record the ups and downs of the past few weeks. You may also want to write down what you have learned about yourself and the nature of life.

Space for general reflection

Week 10

Welcome to Week 10.

How did you get on? Did you complete the small goal from the *work and career* domain? Please take a moment to reflect on your experience. For example, which goal did you choose to complete, why did you choose this goal, how did you feel if you completed the goal, and if you didn't manage to complete the goal then what got in the way?

_____

_____

_____

_____

_____

_____

If you haven't already done so then in the next week please try to complete the bold goal from the *work and career* domain. If you have already completed both the small and bold goals from Week 9 (or if it isn't appropriate to complete the bold goal this week), use the space below to write a couple more goals for this domain to complete over the next week.

🎯 Goal

_____

_____

_____

🎯 Goal

_____

_____

_____

What is Willingness?

Let's start to think about those four ACT processes – willingness, defusion, contact with the present moment and the observing self – that we introduced in Week 8. Perhaps take a look back at them now to refresh your memory – they're on page 51.

We'll begin with willingness. Pursuing as full, rich and meaningful a life as possible while accepting the pain and struggles that inevitably come with it would seem a reasonable trade off. But in everyday life most of us are fine about the first half of that deal and generally less keen about the second half! That is fair enough, as no one wants to experience pain and difficulty.

Yet here's the rub – if we are going to live a rich and fulfilling life, then we cannot avoid the hurt and pain that comes with it. If we want the ups, then we have to be prepared for the downs. If we want to be loved, then we must face the fear of rejection and loss. If we want success, then we must also be ready for failure. We can't have one without the other. This is easy to say and understand, but living it is hard.

In some ways this is the most important message in this diary – life brings both the good and the bad and to live it fully we have to be prepared to embrace both. And that's the deal, whether we like it or not. Rather than trying to get rid of unwanted thoughts and feelings, willingness involves inviting them in, and making a space for them in life (and in the process maybe even discovering that they aren't quite as bad as we initially thought!). This won't sound very appealing on its own, but it opens up the possibility of doing the things that matter, and that is what dignifies our struggles.

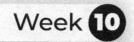

 Summary goal for the week

 27 ACT **Monday**

 28 ACT **Tuesday**

 **1** ACT **Wednesday**

2 ACT  **Thursday**

3 ACT  Friday

4 ACT  Saturday

5 ACT Sunday

*"I like the challenge of trying
different things and wondering whether
I'm going to fall flat on my face."*

Johnny Depp

Week 11

Welcome to Week 11.

How did you get on? Did you complete the bold goal (or an alternative goal) from the *work and career* domain? Please take a moment to reflect on your experience. For example, which goal did you choose to complete, why did you choose this goal, how did you feel if you completed the goal, and if you didn't manage to complete the goal then what got in the way?

Domain 3: Family Relationships

From the values lists in Week 5 and Week 6, which value would you like to bring to life in the domain of *family relationships*?

Please write a very small commitment, which aligns with this value, and is in this domain, to be completed over the next week.

 Goal

Now please write a bold commitment, which aligns with this value, and is in this domain, to be completed over the next two weeks.

 Goal

Please make a note of the barriers (both internal and external) that you think might stop you from completing these goals.

Summary goal for the week

 6 ACT **Monday**

 **7** ACT **Tuesday**

 **8** ACT **Wednesday**

9 ACT  Thursday

10 ACT  Friday

11 ACT  Saturday

12 ACT  Sunday

*"Tennis is just a game,
family is forever."*

Serena Williams

Week 12

Welcome to Week 12.

How did you get on? Did you complete the small goal from the *family relationships* domain? Please take a moment to reflect on your experience. For example, which goal did you choose to complete, why did you choose this goal, how did you feel if you completed the goal, and if you didn't manage to complete the goal then what got in the way?

If you haven't already done so then in the next week please try to complete the bold goal from the *family relationships* domain. If you have already completed both the small and bold goals from Week 11 (or if it isn't appropriate to complete the bold goal this week), use the space below to write a couple more goals for this domain to complete over the next week.

 Goal

 Goal

Exploring Willingness – The Unwelcome Guest

Sometimes metaphors can be really effective in helping us understand certain concepts. See if this metaphor helps you to understand willingness. Meet Sam, like a lot of people he wants to have a party with his friends and enjoy himself. Again, like a lot of people, he wants his guests to have a good time and finds himself feeling anxious about this.

Then just when the party is in full flow Joe shows up. Sam doesn't really like Joe and doesn't want him there. And since his arrival, Sam has felt Joe's been ruining the party. Sam asks Joe to leave but he won't go away, so instead Sam ushers Joe into a back room and guards the door. Only now Sam is missing out on the party too. He longs to re-join it but knows that Joe will follow him and that is the last thing he wants to happen.

Joe is an unwelcome guest, like Sam's anxiety. Sam struggles in vain to get rid of or control his anxious thoughts and feelings, but like Joe they just won't leave. Of course, all the time and effort he puts into trying not to feel anxious means he is less engaged with the party. So what can Sam do? Well, one option is to welcome Joe into the party. Sam will still feel annoyed but at least he can be with his friends rather than waste his time trying to control Joe.

Summary goal for the week

 **13** Monday

---

 **14** Tuesday

---

 **15** Wednesday

16 ACT  Thursday

17 ACT  Friday

18 ACT  Saturday

19 ACT Sunday

"The way I see it, if you want the rainbow, you gotta put up with the rain."

Dolly Parton

Week 13

Welcome to Week 13.

How did you get on? Did you complete the bold goal (or an alternative goal) from the *family relationships* domain? Please take a moment to reflect on your experience. For example, which goal did you choose to complete, why did you choose this goal, how did you feel if you completed the goal, and if you didn't manage to complete the goal then what got in the way?

Domain 4: Education and Learning

From the values lists in Week 5 and Week 6, which value would you like to bring to life in the domain of *education and learning*?

Please write a very small commitment, which aligns with this value, and is in this domain, to be completed over the next week.

 Goal

Now please write a bold commitment, which aligns with this value, and is in this domain, to be completed over the next two weeks.

 Goal

Please make a note of the barriers (both internal and external) that you think might stop you from completing these goals.

March 2023

Summary goal for the week

 **20** Monday

 **21** Tuesday

 **22** Wednesday

 **23** ACT **Thursday**

 **24** ACT **Friday**

 **25** ACT **Saturday**   **26** ACT **Sunday**

> "The whole thing is to learn
> every day, to get brighter and brighter.
> That's what this world is about."
>
> *Jay-Z*

Week 14

Welcome to Week 14.

How did you get on? Did you complete the small goal from the *education and learning* domain? Please take a moment to reflect on your experience. For example, which goal did you choose to complete, why did you choose this goal, how did you feel if you completed the goal, and if you didn't manage to complete the goal then what got in the way?

If you haven't already done so then in the next week please try to complete the bold goal from the *education and learning* domain. If you have already completed both the small and bold goals from Week 13 (or if it isn't appropriate to complete the bold goal this week), use the space below to write a couple more goals for this domain to complete over the next week.

 Goal

 Goal

What is Defusion?

The second ACT process that may be useful in helping us to skilfully manage internal barriers is called defusion. One of the challenges we all face is something called fusion (or sometimes *cognitive fusion*). This is when we become tangled up in our thoughts and believe them to be literally true. Fusion can be problematic because when we really believe our thoughts they can have an undue influence on how we behave. They can almost feel like a command to be followed and this can cause difficulties when they are inaccurate, unhelpful or just plain wrong. For example, if we fuse with the thought *'I can't do that'*, then this is likely to stop us even trying.

Defusion involves a very interesting change of focus. Specifically, instead of questioning the truth of our thoughts, all thoughts are instead evaluated on the basis of their usefulness. In other words, we step back and ask ourselves the question: *'Would acting on this thought help me move in a valued life direction?'*

As an example, the thought *'I'm going to become stressed out if I go into that exam hall'* is probably true. However, it isn't very useful if it stops us from going into the exam hall when our education and careers are important to us. Defusion in this context would involve stepping back from the thought and choosing our behaviour carefully based on our values.

Summary goal for the week

 **27 Monday**

 **28 Tuesday**

 **29 Wednesday**

30 ACT  Thursday

31 ACT  Friday

1 ACT  Saturday

2 ACT Sunday

> "Stay afraid, but do it anyway.
> Just do it and eventually the
> confidence will follow."

Carrie Fisher

Space for general reflection

Use this space to record the ups and downs of the past few weeks. You may also want to write down what you have learned about yourself and the nature of life.

Space for general reflection

Week 15

Welcome to Week 15.

How did you get on? Did you complete the bold goal (or an alternative goal) from the *education and learning* domain? Please take a moment to reflect on your experience. For example, which goal did you choose to complete, why did you choose this goal, how did you feel if you completed the goal, and if you didn't manage to complete the goal then what got in the way?

Domain 5: Intimate Relationships

From the values lists in Week 5 and Week 6, which value would you like to bring to life in the domain of *intimate relationships*?

Please write a very small commitment, which aligns with this value, and is in this domain, to be completed over the next week.

 Goal

Now please write a bold commitment, which aligns with this value, and is in this domain, to be completed over the next two weeks.

 Goal

Please make a note of the barriers (both internal and external) that you think might stop you from completing these goals.

Summary goal for the week

3 **Monday**

4  **Tuesday**

5  **Wednesday**

6 ACT  Thursday

7 ACT  Friday

8 ACT  Saturday

9 ACT  Sunday

*"The best thing to hold onto
in life is each other."*

Audrey Hepburn

Week 16

Welcome to Week 16.

How did you get on? Did you complete the small goal from the *intimate relationships* domain? Please take a moment to reflect on your experience. For example, which goal did you choose to complete, why did you choose this goal, how did you feel if you completed the goal, and if you didn't manage to complete the goal then what got in the way?

If you haven't already done so then in the next week please try to complete the bold goal from the *intimate relationships* domain. If you have already completed both the small and bold goals from Week 15 (or if it isn't appropriate to complete the bold goal this week), use the space below to write a couple more goals for this domain to complete over the next week.

 Goal

 Goal

Exploring Defusion – Having the Thought

Consider this proposition – thoughts, even when they are true, don't have to cause our behaviour. This might sound a little odd at first but try this – think to yourself (or even say out loud) *'Nod your head'*. Repeat this several times and at the same time keep your head still. How did you get on? Did you manage to keep your head still? We bet you did but how is this possible if thoughts control what we do? You can repeat this exercise with any instruction and you will have the same outcome (i.e. thoughts don't have to cause you to behave in certain ways; you can think or say one thing and then act differently).

A great way to reduce the impact that thoughts have on our behaviour is to step back from them by adding the prefix *'I'm having the thought that'* to the thoughts that push us around. This prefix creates a little more space between our thoughts and us, such that we are freer to choose our behaviour.

For example, imagine you had the thought *'I am so bad at first dates that there is no point in ever going on one'*. If you use the prefix it becomes *'I am having the thought that I am so bad at first dates that there is no point in ever going on one'*. Did you notice the shift? In the first instance you probably weren't going to be going on any first dates any time soon, but in the second instance that behaviour felt more likely.

Summary goal for the week

 10 ACT **Monday**

 11 Tuesday

 **12** ACT **Wednesday**

April 2023

Week 16

13 ACT  Thursday

14 ACT  Friday

15 ACT Saturday

16 ACT Sunday

> *"We think too much and feel too little."*
>
> *Charlie Chaplin*

Week 17

Welcome to Week 17.

How did you get on? Did you complete the bold goal (or an alternative goal) from the *intimate relationships* domain? Please take a moment to reflect on your experience. For example, which goal did you choose to complete, why did you choose this goal, how did you feel if you completed the goal, and if you didn't manage to complete the goal then what got in the way?

Domain 6: Self-development and Growth

From the values lists in Week 5 and Week 6, which value would you like to bring to life in the domain of *self-development and growth*?

Please write a very small commitment, which aligns with this value, and is in this domain, to be completed over the next week.

 Goal

Now please write a bold commitment, which aligns with this value, and is in this domain, to be completed over the next two weeks.

 Goal

Please make a note of the barriers (both internal and external) that you think might stop you from completing these goals.

Summary goal for the week

 17 Monday

 18 Tuesday

 **19** Wednesday

20 ACT  Thursday

21 ACT  Friday

22 ACT  Saturday

23 ACT  Sunday

> "We can't become what we need to be by remaining what we are."
> *Oprah Winfrey*

Week 18

Welcome to Week 18.

How did you get on? Did you complete the small goal from the *self-development and growth* domain? Please take a moment to reflect on your experience. For example, which goal did you choose to complete, why did you choose this goal, how did you feel if you completed the goal, and if you didn't manage to complete the goal then what got in the way?

If you haven't already done so then in the next week please try to complete the bold goal from the *self-development and growth* domain. If you have already completed both the small and bold goals from Week 17 (or if it isn't appropriate to complete the bold goal this week), use the space below to write a couple more goals for this domain to complete over the next week.

 Goal

 Goal

What is Contact with the Present Moment?

The third ACT process that can help us to manage thoughts and feelings, and that is often referred to as 'mindfulness' in contemporary culture, is called contact with the present moment. We are so easily dragged into the past or the future that we fail to be in touch with what is going on around us in the present.

Mindfulness involves paying attention to what we are experiencing, on purpose, with an attitude of curiosity. If we are mindful, we notice when our minds have strayed and gently re-orient our attention to what is important in the now.

It sounds simple, and in many ways it is, but it is surprisingly hard to sustain. The reason for this is that the thoughts that go through our minds can pull us away from the present moment and lead us back into the past or forward into the future. However, although mindfulness can be tricky, the good news is that it is a skill, and like all skills, the more we practice it, the better we get.

Summary goal for the week

---

 24 Monday

---

25 Tuesday

 **26** Wednesday

27 ACT  Thursday

28 ACT  Friday

29 ACT  Saturday   **30** ACT  Sunday

"The present is the point
at which time touches eternity."

C.S. Lewis

Space for general reflection

Use this space to record the ups and downs of the past few weeks. You may also want to write down what you have learned about yourself and the nature of life.

Space for general reflection

Week 19

Welcome to Week 19.

How did you get on? Did you complete the bold goal (or an alternative goal) from the *self-development and growth* domain? Please take a moment to reflect on your experience. For example, which goal did you choose to complete, why did you choose this goal, how did you feel if you completed the goal, and if you didn't manage to complete the goal then what got in the way?

Domain 7: Recreation and Leisure

From the values lists in Week 5 and Week 6, which value would you like to bring to life in the domain of *recreation and leisure*?

Please write a very small commitment, which aligns with this value, and is in this domain, to be completed over the next week.

 Goal

Now please write a bold commitment, which aligns with this value, and is in this domain, to be completed over the next two weeks.

 Goal

Please make a note of the barriers (both internal and external) that you think might stop you from completing these goals.

Summary goal for the week

 **❶ Monday**

 **❷ Tuesday**

 **❸ Wednesday**

 4 ACT **Thursday**

 5 ACT **Friday**

 6 ACT **Saturday**

 7 ACT **Sunday**

"The bow cannot always stand bent, nor can human frailty subsist without some lawful recreation."

Miguel de Cervantes

Week 20

Welcome to Week 20.

How did you get on? Did you complete the small goal from the *recreation and leisure* domain? Please take a moment to reflect on your experience. For example, which goal did you choose to complete, why did you choose this goal, how did you feel if you completed the goal, and if you didn't manage to complete the goal then what got in the way?

If you haven't already done so then in the next week please try to complete the bold goal from the *recreation and leisure* domain. If you have already completed both the small and bold goals from Week 19 (or if it isn't appropriate to complete the bold goal this week), use the space below to write a couple more goals for this domain to complete over the next week.

 Goal

 Goal

Exploring Contact with the Present Moment – Breathing

Have you ever tried to train a puppy to sit? If not, let us tell you what happens. Every time you say *'sit'*, the puppy runs off. When this happens we do not get angry or cross with the puppy because they are just doing what puppies do. Our minds are like puppies (they keep running off to different places). Contrary to common assumptions, the point of mindfulness isn't to train our puppy-like mind to sit and stay, it is to simply notice that we have puppy-like minds that will probably be puppy-like forever. Once we begin to notice where our puppy-like minds wander off to (into thoughts or memories), then we will be better able to reorient our attention back to the present moment.

Let's try a mindfulness of breath exercise to introduce you to your puppy-like mind. All you have to do in this task is to breathe in and out ten times. However, as you do this, we want you to try to bring all of your attention to the process of breathing (i.e. only think about your breath). Each time that your mind wanders, notice this has happened and gently reconnect with the experience of your breath, like the rise and fall of your chest or the in and out movement of your stomach.

How did you get on? We'd bet that your mind strayed to many different thoughts about the past and the future, and in doing so, introduced you to your puppy like mind and to the purpose of mindfulness: to re-contact the present moment when our minds have wandered.

Summary goal for the week

 **8** ## Monday

---

 **9** ## Tuesday

---

 **10** ## Wednesday

11 ACT  **Thursday**

12 ACT  **Friday**

13 ACT  **Saturday**

14 ACT **Sunday**

> "He lives most life whoever
> breathes most air."
>
> *Elizabeth Barrett Browning*

Week 21

Welcome to Week 21.

How did you get on? Did you complete the bold goal (or an alternative goal) from the *recreation and leisure* domain? Please take a moment to reflect on your experience. For example, which goal did you choose to complete, why did you choose this goal, how did you feel if you completed the goal, and if you didn't manage to complete the goal then what got in the way?

Domain 8: Spirituality

From the values lists in Week 5 and Week 6, which value would you like to bring to life in the domain of *spirituality*? Sometimes, people do not deem spirituality as an important domain. If that is the case for you then please complete this page with more general values and goals in mind.

Please write a very small commitment, which aligns with this value, and is in this domain, to be completed over the next week.

 Goal

Now please write a bold commitment, which aligns with this value, and is in this domain, to be completed over the next two weeks.

 Goal

Please make a note of the barriers (both internal and external) that you think might stop you from completing these goals.

Summary goal for the week

15 Monday

16 Tuesday

17 Wednesday

18 ACT Thursday

19 ACT  Friday

20 ACT  Saturday

21 ACT Sunday

"I have learned the importance of keeping spiritual life and professional life balanced."

Tiger Woods

Week 22

Welcome to Week 22.

How did you get on? Did you complete the small goal from the *spirituality* domain? Please take a moment to reflect on your experience. For example, which goal did you choose to complete, why did you choose this goal, how did you feel if you completed the goal, and if you didn't manage to complete the goal then what got in the way?

_____

_____

_____

_____

_____

_____

If you haven't already done so then in the next week please try to complete the bold goal from the *spirituality* domain. If you have already completed both the small and bold goals from Week 21 (or if it isn't appropriate to complete the bold goal this week), use the space below to write a couple more goals for this domain to complete over the next week.

 Goal

_____

_____

 Goal

_____

_____

What is the Observing Self?

The last ACT process that can help you to manage tricky thoughts and feelings is called the observing self. In ACT there is an old saying: *'Kill your self every day'*. Of course, this doesn't mean literally to kill yourself; it means that over time we build stories about *'who we are'*, but that often these stories can hold us back. Therefore, kill your stories about *'who you are'* every day so that you can escape their grasp.

When we start to think about who we are in this way, the impossible becomes possible:

- If we kill the self-story that we are not clever enough to go for a promotion, we get to try for that promotion.
- If we kill the self-story that we are not mentally tough enough to lose weight, we get to go to the gym and try.
- If we kill the self-story that we are not a sociable sort of person, we get to try to connect with people.

The observing self, rather than being caught up in our stories, simply watches them. It can be thought of as a container for all of our experiences, the stable and ongoing sense of 'I' that exists independently of the stories that our minds might feed us. When we begin to see ourselves like this then the extent that our stories define us will fall away and we will be more able to choose better ways to behave.

Summary goal for the week

 Monday

 Tuesday

 Wednesday

25 ACT  Thursday

26 ACT  Friday

27 ACT  Saturday

28 ACT Sunday

"If only we could pull out
our brains and use only our eyes."

Pablo Picasso

Space for general reflection

Use this space to record the ups and downs of the past few weeks. You may also want to write down what you have learned about yourself and the nature of life.

Space for general reflection

Week 23

Welcome to Week 23.

How did you get on? Did you complete the bold goal (or an alternative goal) from the *spirituality* domain? Please take a moment to reflect on your experience. For example, which goal did you choose to complete, why did you choose this goal, how did you feel if you completed the goal, and if you didn't manage to complete the goal then what got in the way?

Domain 9: Community and Citizenship

From the values lists in Week 5 and Week 6, which value would you like to bring to life in the domain of *community and citizenship*?

Please write a very small commitment, which aligns with this value, and is in this domain, to be completed over the next week.

 Goal

Now please write a bold commitment, which aligns with this value, and is in this domain, to be completed over the next two weeks.

 Goal

Please make a note of the barriers (both internal and external) that you think might stop you from completing these goals.

May 2023

🎯 Summary goal for the week

✓

29 Monday

30  Tuesday

31  Wednesday

June 2023

1 ACT  **Thursday**

2 ACT  Friday

3 ACT  Saturday

4 ACT Sunday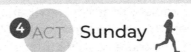

"I alone cannot change the world, but I can cast a stone across the waters to create many ripples."

Mother Teresa

Week 24

Welcome to Week 24.

How did you get on? Did you complete the small goal from the *community and citizenship* domain? Please take a moment to reflect on your experience. For example, which goal did you choose to complete, why did you choose this goal, how did you feel if you completed the goal, and if you didn't manage to complete the goal then what got in the way?

If you haven't already done so then in the next week please try to complete the bold goal from the *community and citizenship* domain. If you have already completed both the small and bold goals from Week 23 (or if it isn't appropriate to complete the bold goal this week), use the space below to write a couple more goals for this domain to complete over the next week.

 Goal

 Goal

Exploring the Observing Self – The Sky and the Weather

A metaphor that nicely illustrates the observing self (which can be a difficult concept to understand) is the relationship between the sky and the weather.

You are like the sky. Your thoughts and feelings are like the weather. The weather changes constantly. Sometimes there is sunshine. However, sometimes there are clouds, wind, rain or storms. Your thoughts and feelings are like this. Sometimes they are happy. However, sometimes they are sad, angry, worried or anxious. There are a couple of important things to know about the relationship between the sky and the weather. Firstly, the weather can never hurt the sky in the same way that your thoughts and feelings can never physically hurt you. Secondly, the sky can always hold the weather no matter how bad it is. You are the same: you can make room for tricky thoughts and feelings no matter how bad they seem.

Sometimes we forget that the sky is there – perhaps it is hard to see the sky through the weather. When this happens it is easy to believe that our thoughts and our self-stories are the sky. They are us. However, every now and then you notice the sky; stable, broad, limitless and pure. The observing self involves learning to access the sky more, and seeing it as a place where we can make room for, and watch, difficult thoughts and feelings about ourselves, rather than be defined by them.

Summary goal for the week

 5 **Monday**

 **6** **Tuesday**

7 **Wednesday**

June 2023

8 ACT  Thursday

9 ACT  Friday

10 ACT  Saturday

11 ACT  Sunday

> "Be comforted, dear soul,
> there is always light behind clouds."
> *Louisa May Alcott*

Week 25

Welcome to Week 25.

How did you get on? Did you complete the bold goal (or an alternative goal) from the *community and citizenship* domain? Please take a moment to reflect on your experience. For example, which goal did you choose to complete, why did you choose this goal, how did you feel if you completed the goal, and if you didn't manage to complete the goal then what got in the way?

Domain 10: Health and Physical Wellbeing

From the values lists in Week 5 and Week 6, which value would you like to bring to life in the domain of *health and physical wellbeing*?

Please write a very small commitment, which aligns with this value, and is in this domain, to be completed over the next week.

 Goal

Now please write a bold commitment, which aligns with this value, and is in this domain, to be completed over the next two weeks.

 Goal

Please make a note of the barriers (both internal and external) that you think might stop you from completing these goals.

Summary goal for the week

---

12  **Monday**

---

13 **Tuesday**

---

14 **Wednesday**

June 2023

Week **25**

15 ACT  **Thursday**

16 ACT  **Friday**

17 ACT  **Saturday**

18 ACT  **Sunday**

> "A healthy attitude is
> contagious but don't wait to catch
> it from others. Be a carrier."
>
> *Tom Stoppard*

Week 26

Welcome to Week 26.

How did you get on? Did you complete the small goal from the *health and physical wellbeing* domain? Please take a moment to reflect on your experience. For example, which goal did you choose to complete, why did you choose this goal, how did you feel if you completed the goal, and if you didn't manage to complete the goal then what got in the way?

If you haven't already done so then in the next week please try to complete the bold goal from the *health and physical wellbeing* domain. If you have already completed both the small and bold goals from Week 25 (or if it isn't appropriate to complete the bold goal this week), use the space below to write a couple more goals for this domain to complete over the next week.

 Goal

 Goal

What is the Hexaflex?

We're halfway through the year! We hope that three things are happening for you. Firstly, we hope that bringing a greater focus to values and goals is positively impacting your life. Secondly, we hope you see that values exist independent of the goals you set (i.e. values can trickle into your life as and when the situation calls for it). Make a note when this happens! And thirdly, we hope that you are beginning to understand what ACT is all about.

In fact, you've now been properly introduced to the six parts that comprise the ACT model. On page 15 we saw how these could be tied together in a simple diagram called *The Triflex*. Another way in which the six core processes are often depicted is via *The Hexaflex*, which is shown below. The idea is that you can use any or all of the four processes on the left-hand side of the hexaflex to help you more skilfully relate to your thoughts and feelings, such that you are then freer to move towards your values/goals.

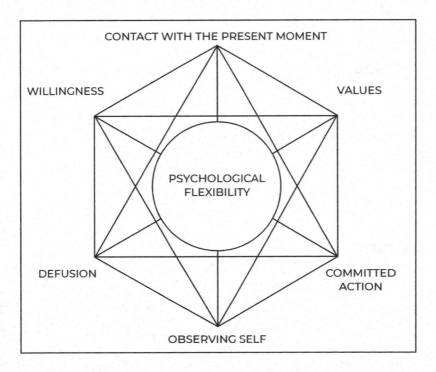

© Steven C. Hayes, adapted.

Summary goal for the week

---

 19 ACT **Monday**

---

20 **Tuesday**

 **21** ACT **Wednesday**

June 2023

22 ACT  **Thursday**

23 ACT  Friday

24 ACT  Saturday

25 ACT Sunday

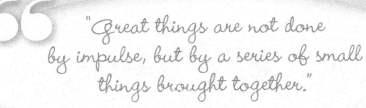

"*Great things are not done
by impulse, but by a series of small
things brought together.*"

George Eliot

Week 27

Welcome to Week 27.

How did you get on? Did you complete the bold goal (or an alternative goal) from the *health and physical wellbeing* domain? Please take a moment to reflect on your experience. For example, which goal did you choose to complete, why did you choose this goal, how did you feel if you completed the goal, and if you didn't manage to complete the goal then what got in the way?

A Values Exercise – Writing a Eulogy

Now that we've explored values across various domains we're going to ask you to complete a powerful values exercise in the hope that it can clarify your most important values. In fact, you may need the core ACT processes detailed in the hexaflex to help you manage the discomfort that this exercise can provoke (note: keep yourself safe – if you don't fancy this exercise then don't do it).

Imagine for a second that you had died. And that at the funeral, the three most important people in your life stood up and spoke about you. In an absolutely ideal world, what would you like those people to say? Please write this below.

In your answer, you will have detailed the sort of qualities you'd like to embody in this world (or your values). Please choose one and write a value-consistent goal below that you can complete over the next week.

 Goal

June 2023

 Summary goal for the week

---

26 Monday

---

27  Tuesday

---

28 Wednesday

29 ACT  Thursday

30 ACT  Friday

1 ACT  Saturday

2 ACT Sunday

"In the final analysis,
we count for something only because
of the essential that we embody."

Carl Jung

Space for general reflection

Use this space to record the ups and downs of the past few weeks. You may also want to write down what you have learned about yourself and the nature of life.

Space for general reflection

Week 28

Welcome to Week 28.

How did you get on? Did you complete the goal from the eulogy exercise? Please take a moment to reflect on your experience. For example, what was the goal, why did you choose it, how did you feel if you completed it, and if you didn't complete it then what got in the way?

Please now return to your answer from the eulogy exercise in Week 27 and record another values-consistent goal below, to complete in the next week.

🎯 Goal

Introducing Self-Compassion

The thing about setting goals, both in the context of this diary and in the context of our lives more broadly, is that often we fail to complete them! We are going to assume that this has happened many times already this year for you. When we do fail to meet our goals we human beings tend to pick up a big stick and hit ourselves with it, metaphorically speaking. Not only that, but while we are busy beating ourselves up we somehow manage to give up on our goals, as if they are lost forever. For many of us this is all too familiar, but is there a better way, you could even say a more useful way, to respond to ourselves when we mess up? How about a bit of self-compassion?

Compassion is comprised of two distinct parts – it's about being sensitive to other people's distress *and* being motivated to do something about it. When we have compassion, we feel another's pain and make efforts to support them with it. Self-compassion is essentially the same process; only it involves acting in this way towards ourselves. It involves noticing our critical minds, our pain or aspects of ourselves that we don't like and responding with kindness, patience and understanding.

In other words, instead of ignoring our suffering or just relentlessly criticising ourselves for our inadequacies, we try to ask the following question when we have failed *'What can I do to care for myself, or be kind to myself, right now?'*

Summary goal for the week

 **3** **Monday**

 **4** **Tuesday**

 **5** **Wednesday**

6 ACT  **Thursday**

7 ACT  Friday

8 ACT  Saturday

9 ACT  Sunday

> "Love yourself first and
> everything else falls into line."
> *Lucille Ball*

Week 29

Welcome to Week 29.

How did you get on? Did you complete another goal from the eulogy exercise? Please take a moment to reflect on your experience. For example, what was the goal, why did you choose it, how did you feel if you completed it, and if you didn't complete it then what got in the way?

_____

_____

_____

_____

_____

_____

_____

_____

_____

_____

_____

_____

For the final time, please now return to your answer from the eulogy exercise in Week 27 and record another values-consistent goal below, to complete in the next week.

 Goal

_____

_____

_____

Exploring Self-Compassion – Helping a Child

Interestingly, it seems easier to be compassionate than to be self-compassionate. What we are wondering, therefore, is whether it is possible to extend the same kindness and support to yourself that you would give so easily to someone you love? This exercise aims to explore that question.

Imagine that you're a teacher in a primary school. One rainy Tuesday morning it's your turn to do playground duty. As you walk around the playground, you notice that one particular little girl is running around too vigorously given the wet conditions. As you make your way over to speak to her, the girl falls really hard on the ground, grazing her knees, hands and nose. She cries and cries.

How would you react? What would you do? Really try to picture it. You might cuddle the little girl. You might tell her that everything is going to be ok. You might make a joke to cheer her up. You might miss your own lunch to sit with her while the nurse begins treatment.

It is amazing how compassionate we can be to other people, but what if that little girl is a metaphor for you in this world? What if you are picking up grazes (failures and mistakes) as you try to manage the trickiness of life? Can you treat yourself with the same kindness that you would so easily give to this little girl?

July 2023

 Summary goal for the week

 **10** Monday

 **11** Tuesday

 **12** Wednesday

July 2023

13 ACT  Thursday

14 ACT  Friday

15 ACT  Saturday

16 ACT  Sunday

"All that matters is kindness and the capacity to recognise the existence of people other than you."

Zadie Smith

Week 30

Welcome to Week 30.

How did you get on? Did you complete a third and final goal from the eulogy exercise? Please take a moment to reflect on your experience. For example, what was the goal, why did you choose it, how did you feel if you completed it, and if you didn't complete it then what got in the way?

In the next few weeks, we'd like you to add another layer to your experience of values by writing personal values statements across four broad areas of your life. In between writing these, we'll introduce you to the notion of experiential avoidance, which forms an important part of the ACT rationale.

Personal Values Statement: Health

Is your *health* important to you? If so, why? Possibly because being healthy will allow you to travel, will allow you to do sport or will allow you to spend time with the people that you love? Have a think about which values might be useful to you in this area, and write a values statement below. An example of a values statement might be *'My health is important to me because it will allow me to play sport as I grow older. Consequently, I would like to be patient and persistent as I attempt to become fitter'*.

Personal Values Statement:

Now, in the spaces below, please record six goals that you can complete, short-term and long-term, which would bring you closer to your personal values statement in the area of *health*. Try to complete one or more of these goals in the next week.

Goal 1

Goal 2

Goal 3

Goal 4

Goal 5

Goal 6

Summary goal for the week

 **17** Monday

 **18** Tuesday

 **19** Wednesday

20 ACT  Thursday

21 ACT  Friday

22 ACT Saturday

23 ACT Sunday

> *"Our bodies are our gardens
> — our wills are our gardeners."*
> **William Shakespeare**

Week 31

Welcome to Week 31.

How did you get on? Did you complete any goals related to your personal values statement in the area of *health*? Please take a moment to reflect on your experience. For example, how did you feel if you completed any of the goals, and if you didn't complete some of them then what got in the way?

Please now return to Week 30 (where you wrote a personal values statement in the area of *health*), pick one or more further goals to complete in the next week and write them in the space below.

🎯 Goal

🎯 Goal

Introducing Experiential Avoidance

Here is a truth that is not often told – life is tough. No doubt there are times when things are great and we feel content and happy, but often this is not the case. Worries, stresses, fears, regrets, aches and pains all too frequently hold our attention. The carving up of human suffering into conditions can give the impression that these problems are individually rare. However, when we group them together we see that it is quite the opposite – suffering is commonplace. Indeed, it is quite normal.

The problem is human language. Give an animal food, water and social contact in a safe and comfortable place and they will be content. But this is not so for human beings. Even when surrounded by abundance, thanks to our language we can feel scared, sad, concerned or confused at any time by just thinking about certain things. Right now, in this moment, you could bring sorrow into your life by simply recalling a painful memory or imagining an unwanted future.

It would be great if we could turn off our thinking from time to time, so as to avoid the suffering it can bring. However, experiential avoidance, the attempted removal of unwanted thoughts and feelings from our minds, not only doesn't work but often leads to more problems, as we will explore in the next few weeks.

Summary goal for the week

 24 **Monday**

 25 **Tuesday**

 26 **Wednesday**

27 ACT  Thursday

28 ACT  Friday

29 ACT Saturday   **30** ACT Sunday

> "*You cannot find peace by avoiding life.*"
>
> *Virginia Woolf*

Space for general reflection

Use this space to record the ups and downs of the past few weeks. You may also want to write down what you have learned about yourself and the nature of life.

Space for general reflection

Week 32

Welcome to Week 32.

How did you get on? Did you complete another goal from the personal values statement in the area of *health*? Please take a moment to reflect on your experience. For example, how did you feel if you completed any of the goals, and if you didn't complete some of them then what got in the way?

Personal Values Statement: Work

Is your *work* important to you? If so, why? Possibly because it brings you fulfilment or because it allows you to provide for your family? Have a think about which values might be useful to you in this area, and write a values statement below. An example of a values statement might be *'My work is important to me because it allows me to contribute to the lives of others. Consequently, I would like to be creative and enthusiastic as I move forward with my career'*.

Personal Values Statement:

Now, in the spaces below, please record six goals that you can complete, short-term and long-term, which would bring you closer to your personal values statement in the area of *work*. Try to complete one or more of these goals in the next week.

Goal 1

Goal 2

Goal 3

Goal 4

Goal 5

Goal 6

July/August 2023

 Summary goal for the week

31 Monday

1 **Tuesday**

2 Wednesday

3 ACT  Thursday

4 ACT  Friday

5 ACT  Saturday

6 ACT Sunday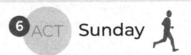

"Nothing will work unless you do."

Maya Angelou

Week 33

Welcome to Week 33.

How did you get on? Did you complete a goal related to your personal values statement in the area of *work*? Please take a moment to reflect on your experience. For example, how did you feel if you completed any of the goals, and if you didn't complete some of them then what got in the way?

Please now return to Week 32 (where you wrote a personal values statement in the area of *work*), pick one or more further goals to complete in the next week and write them in the space below.

 Goal

 Goal

Exploring Experiential Avoidance – The White Bear

What would you do if you felt cold, were caught in the rain, or had a stone in your shoe? Most probably you would act in ways that reduced the discomfort you were experiencing. You might, for example, put on a jumper, put up an umbrella, remove the stone or even hop on one leg. Your actions would depend on your particular circumstances but in general they would all have the same aim – to reduce, stop or avoid the discomfort. Avoiding or reducing negative, painful or unpleasant experiences can be a good survival strategy, as it lessens our exposure to events that might harm us. It's easy to see why acting to avoid negative events makes sense and is hard-wired into us by our evolutionary past.

However, a problem emerges when we apply this same strategy to the world inside our skin because we just don't have the same level of control over our internal world as we do over events in the external world. To illustrate how little control we sometimes have over our minds, please complete this popular exercise: *for one minute, try your best to not think about a white bear, if you do think about it then leave a mark on a piece of paper.*

How did you get on? Most people report seeing the dreaded bear on many occasions and in doing so learn that trying our best to avoid certain thoughts may be a futile activity.

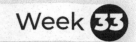

August 2023

Week 33

 Summary goal for the week

 7 ACT **Monday**

8 ACT **Tuesday**

9 ACT **Wednesday**

August 2023

Week **33**

10 ACT  Thursday

11 ACT  Friday

12 ACT Saturday

13 ACT Sunday

"Do not anticipate trouble or worry about what may never happen. Keep in the sunlight."

Benjamin Franklin

Week 34

Welcome to Week 34.

How did you get on? Did you complete another goal from the personal values statement in the area of *work*? Please take a moment to reflect on your experience. For example, how did you feel if you completed any of the goals, and if you didn't complete some of them then what got in the way?

Personal Values Statement: Leisure

Is *leisure* important to you? If so, why? Possibly because it helps you to have fun or because it allows you to spend time with friends? Have a think about which values might be useful to you in this area, and write a values statement below. An example of a values statement might be *'My leisure is important to me because it allows me to appreciate spending time with my friends. Consequently, I would like to make time for leisure, and bring humour and challenge to my leisure activities'.*

Personal Values Statement:

Now, in the spaces below, please record six goals that you can complete, short-term and long-term, which would bring you closer to your personal values statement in the area of *leisure*. Try to complete one or more of these goals in the next week.

Goal 1

Goal 2

Goal 3

Goal 4

Goal 5

Goal 6

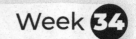
 Summary goal for the week

 14 Monday

 15 Tuesday

 16 Wednesday

August 2023

17 ACT  Thursday

18 ACT  Friday

19 ACT  Saturday

20 ACT Sunday

> "If adults are not enjoying something they're doing in their leisure time, they should stop doing it."
>
> *Nick Hornby*

Week 35

Welcome to Week 35.

How did you get on? Did you complete a goal related to your personal values statement in the area of *leisure*? Please take a moment to reflect on your experience. For example, how did you feel if you completed any of the goals, and if you didn't complete some of them then what got in the way?

Please now return to Week 34 (where you wrote a personal values statement in the area of *leisure*), pick one or more further goals to complete in the next week and write them in the space below.

🎯 Goal

🎯 Goal

Exploring Experiential Avoidance – A Crucial Side Effect

In addition to being a futile activity in and of itself, a crucial side effect of avoidance is that it tends to impact our behaviour in negative ways. Specifically, efforts to avoid unwanted thoughts and feelings can lead to avoiding the situations that give rise to them. While this can seem like it solves the initial problem – avoidance of the unwanted thoughts or feelings – we are restricting our lives in the process, which can have a major impact on our wider sense of fulfilment.

For example, if meeting other people makes us anxious, then we could avoid places where they might be. Sounds like a good solution but it also means that our lives become smaller, maybe even limited just to our home. Whilst this might sound extreme, there are thousands of people for whom this is a daily reality. They might not be fully aware of it, but the solution to their first problem has created a second, bigger problem.

When avoidance of discomfort is our primary aim, the amount of value-consistent activities that we can engage in will grow smaller and smaller. This is because sometimes the things that are most important to us are also the things that bring us pain or discomfort.

Summary goal for the week

21 **Monday**

22  **Tuesday**

23 **Wednesday**

August 2023

24 ACT  Thursday

25 ACT  Friday

26 ACT  Saturday

27 ACT  Sunday

> "He who replies to words of
> doubt doth put the light of knowledge out."
>
> *William Blake*

Week 36

Welcome to Week 36.

How did you get on? Did you complete another goal from the personal values statement in the area of *leisure*? Please take a moment to reflect on your experience. For example, how did you feel if you completed any of the goals, and if you didn't complete some of them then what got in the way?

Personal Values Statement: Relationships

Are *relationships* important to you? If so, why? Possibly because the feeling of human connection brings you meaning or perhaps having healthy relationships allow you to complete other goals? Have a think about which values might be useful to you in this area, and write a values statement below. An example of a values statement might be *'My relationships are important to me because of the energy and love that they bring me. Consequently, I would like to bring kindness, patience and positivity to the people in my life'.*

Personal Values Statement:

Now, in the spaces below, please record 6 goals that you can complete, short-term and long-term, which would bring you closer to your personal values statement in the area of *relationships*. Try to complete one or more of these goals in the next week.

Goal 1

Goal 2

Goal 3

Goal 4

Goal 5

Goal 6

August 2023

 Summary goal for the week

28 ACT **Monday**

29 ACT **Tuesday**

30 ACT **Wednesday**

31 ACT  Thursday

1 ACT  Friday

2 ACT  Saturday

3 ACT  Sunday

"A dream you dream alone is only a dream. A dream you dream together is reality."

Yoko Ono

Space for general reflection

Use this space to record the ups and downs of the past few weeks. You may also want to write down what you have learned about yourself and the nature of life.

Space for general reflection

Week 37

Welcome to Week 37.

How did you get on? Did you complete a goal related to your personal values statement in the area of *relationships*? Please take a moment to reflect on your experience. For example, how did you feel if you completed any of the goals, and if you didn't complete some of them then what got in the way?

_____

_____

_____

_____

_____

_____

_____

Please now return to Week 36 (where you wrote a personal values statement in the area of *relationships*), pick one or more further goals to complete in the next week and write them in the space below.

🎯 Goal

_____

_____

_____

🎯 Goal

_____

_____

Exploring Experiential Avoidance – A Ball in the Water

A perfect metaphor for illustrating the impact of engaging in experiential avoidance involves trying to keep a ball submerged underwater.

Imagine that a ball represents your negative thoughts and feelings. You really don't want to have these thoughts and feelings so you try to get rid of them by holding them under the water. As you hold the ball under the water you notice three things. Firstly, that even with your best efforts the ball continues to pop out of the water. Unwanted thoughts and feelings are like this; they are very difficult to suppress. Secondly, you notice that your arms are hurting from trying to hold the ball under the water. Attempted suppression takes a lot of effort. Thirdly, you realise that by fighting with the ball you are missing out on playing games with your friends. Attempted suppression can spill over into valued activities.

To summarise experiential avoidance – while wanting to avoid painful and/ or discomforting internal experiences is quite natural, doing so often has negative consequences (i.e. it doesn't work, it takes a lot of effort and it can stop you from engaging in valued activities). It is for this reason that ACT is an approach that involves doing the exact opposite of avoidance.

September 2023

 Summary goal for the week

 **4** ACT **Monday**

 **5** ACT **Tuesday**

 **6** ACT **Wednesday**

September 2023

7 ACT  **Thursday**

8 ACT  **Friday**

9 ACT  **Saturday**

10 ACT  **Sunday**

"People become attached to their burdens sometimes more than their burdens are attached to them."

George Bernard Shaw

Week 38

Welcome to Week 38.

How did you get on? Did you complete another goal from the personal values statement in the area of *relationships*? Please take a moment to reflect on your experience. For example, how did you feel if you completed any of the goals, and if you didn't complete some of them then what got in the way?

Giving You The Reins

Throughout this diary we have gradually asked you to delve deeper and deeper into your values. At this moment, therefore, you should have a fairly good idea of which domains in your life are most important, and what qualities you would like to turn into action on this earth.

From this point forward, in addition to describing some helpful ACT metaphors across each domain of the hexaflex, we are going to be less prescriptive about how you bring your values to life. Instead, we are going go full circle by asking you again the very first question that you saw in this diary.

What do you want to achieve in the next few months? In the space below please record some values and goals that are important to you at this point in your life, and detail how you might move towards one or more of those goals in the next week.

🎯 Goal

🎯 Goal

🎯 Goal

Summary goal for the week

 **11** **Monday**

 **12** **Tuesday**

 **13** **Wednesday**

14 ACT  **Thursday**

15 ACT  Friday

16 ACT  **Saturday**

17 ACT Sunday

*"If you love life,
don't waste time, for time is
what life is made up of."*

Bruce Lee

Week 39

Welcome to Week 39.

How did you get on? Did you make progress? Take a moment to reflect on your experience. Were your behaviours this week generally value consistent or value inconsistent?

Record some values and goals that are important to you and which you can try to complete in the next week.

🎯 Goal

🎯 Goal

Exploring Willingness – Quicksand

The thing about avoidance is that it comes so naturally to us. For example, if there is danger in the outside world then avoidance is a good problem solving strategy. However, that same strategy, when applied to the internal world of our thoughts and feelings, doesn't work. But what might? Well, it is easy enough for us to yell the word *'willingness'* at you right now, but there is no doubt that willingness can feel like an odd thing to do at first, as the quicksand metaphor aims to illustrate.

If you are ever stuck in quicksand then every bone in your body will urge you to keep moving your arms and your legs in an attempt to get out. In other words, your instinct will tell you to struggle with the quicksand. However, the problem with struggling in quicksand is that the more you struggle and fight to get out the more quickly you will get sucked in. In fact, the only way to escape from quicksand, as unnatural as it may feel, is to stop struggling. What you are supposed to do is lie back, spread out your body and be as still as possible.

Willingness to experience unwanted thoughts and feelings is a little bit like this. Our every instinct tells us to get rid of them. However, struggling with our unwanted thoughts and feelings won't work in the same way that struggling with quicksand won't work. Your better option, even though it may feel unnatural, is to take them with you.

September 2023

 Summary goal for the week

---

 18 Monday

---

 19 Tuesday

 **20** Wednesday

21 ACT  Thursday

22 ACT  Friday

23 ACT Saturday

24 ACT  Sunday

*"Feelings can't be ignored,
no matter how unjust
or ungrateful they seem."*
Anne Frank

Week 40

Welcome to Week 40.

How did you get on? Did you make progress? Take a moment to reflect on your experience. Were your behaviours this week generally value consistent or value inconsistent?

Record some values and goals that are important to you and which you can try to complete in the next week.

🎯 Goal

🎯 Goal

Exploring Willingness Further – Tug-of-War with a Monster

Do you know what a tug-of-war contest is? Team A holds one end of a rope, Team B holds the other end and between the two teams there is a large puddle of dirty water. One metaphor about a tug-of-war contest can be useful in helping us to think about willingness.

Imagine you are in a tug-of-war contest with a big, ugly monster. Between the two of you is a large and seemingly bottomless hole. If you lose the contest you will surely die. So you start pulling. You look up to see the monster holding the rope with just one hand despite the fact that you are pulling as hard as you can. The monster then decides to take the contest a bit more seriously. He begins pulling and you find yourself moving closer and closer to the hole of death. You pull harder, but he is stronger, so what can you do?

ACT teaches us that we don't need to change our thoughts and feelings. We can instead develop the willingness to experience them. We can acknowledge their existence and get on with the act of living. In other words, ACT helps us to see that we no longer have to win a tug-of-war contest with our monsters; we can learn to drop the rope.

Summary goal for the week

 **25** Monday

 **26** Tuesday

 **27** Wednesday

 **28** ACT **Thursday**

 **29** ACT **Friday**

 **30** ACT **Saturday**   **1** ACT **Sunday**

> "I had no idea that history was
> being made. I was just tired of giving up."
>
> *Rosa Parks*

Space for general reflection

Use this space to record the ups and downs of the past few weeks. You may also want to write down what you have learned about yourself and the nature of life.

Space for general reflection

Week 41

Welcome to Week 41.

How did you get on? Did you make progress? Take a moment to reflect on your experience. Were your behaviours this week generally value consistent or value inconsistent?

Record some values and goals that are important to you and which you can try to complete in the next week.

🎯 Goal

🎯 Goal

Exploring Defusion – Leaves on a Stream

Defusion is all about getting better at watching and noticing our thoughts. A great way to improve defusion skills is via a meditation type exercise that requires you to watch your thoughts like you would watch leaves on a stream. Below are some instructions for how to do this:

1. Close your eyes and picture yourself being sat next to a stream on a warm summer's day.

2. Now, for three minutes, watch any thoughts that pop into your mind.

3. As you notice a thought, pick it up and place it gently on a leaf that is making its way down the stream.

4. The leaf may hang around for a little bit. That's fine. Don't force its movement. If it hangs around then continue to watch it, if it floats away then watch it float away. Your only job is to notice it.

5. Do this with every thought that you notice, positive and negative.

6. If your mind seems to stop giving you thoughts then wait a while and they will come back. When they do, place them on a leaf.

7. If your mind says *'I'm rubbish at this'* or *'This is a silly exercise'* then place those thoughts on a leaf too.

8. Don't slow down or speed up the leaves. Your job here is only to notice.

9. You will get pulled out of the exercise, at times. When that happens, simply place the next thought on a leaf and continue.

Summary goal for the week

 **2** Monday

 **3** Tuesday

 4 Wednesday

5 ACT  Thursday

6 ACT  Friday

7 ACT  Saturday   **8** ACT Sunday

> *"Turn off your mind,*
> *relax, and float downstream."*
>
> *John Lennon*

Week 42

Welcome to Week 42.

How did you get on? Did you make progress? Take a moment to reflect on your experience. Were your behaviours this week generally value consistent or value inconsistent?

Record some values and goals that are important to you and which you can try to complete in the next week.

🎯 Goal

🎯 Goal

Exploring Defusion Further – Hands as Thoughts

In addition to watching our thoughts, a key part of defusion is experiencing how being wrapped up in them can negatively impact our daily life. The *'Hands as Thoughts'* metaphor illustrates this idea.

Bring your hands up to your face and fix them in front of your eyes. What happens to your view of the room when you do this? Is it difficult to concentrate on a particular task? Would you be able to use your hands for anything else whilst they are fixed in front of your face like this? Your thoughts can be like this. When they are very close to us, right up in front of our eyes, they can have a negative impact on us. Specifically, when certain thoughts dominate our existence it can be difficult to notice things going on around us, it can be difficult to concentrate on a particular task, and it can be difficult to take effective action.

Now put your hands in your lap. The thoughts are still there, but you now have a bit of distance from them. As a result you are in a better position to interact with the things going on around you, you are in a better position to concentrate on the tasks in front of you and you are in a better position to act in an effective way.

October 2023

 Summary goal for the week

 9 ACT **Monday**

 10 ACT **Tuesday**

11 ACT **Wednesday**

October 2023

12 ACT **Thursday**

13 ACT **Friday**

14 ACT **Saturday**

15 ACT **Sunday**

> "It's hard to see things when
> you're too close. Take a step back and look."
>
> *Bob Ross*

Week 43

Welcome to Week 43.

How did you get on? Did you make progress? Take a moment to reflect on your experience. Were your behaviours this week generally value consistent or value inconsistent?

Record some values and goals that are important to you and which you can try to complete in the next week.

🎯 Goal

🎯 Goal

Exploring Mindfulness – The Body Scan

Mindfulness isn't about your ability to focus on your breath per se. Instead, formal mindfulness exercises are used to train a key skill – the ability to bring your attention back to the present moment when your mind has wandered – so that you can use that skill in situations that call for it. Like mindfulness of breath, the body scan is another popular formal mindfulness exercise, which involves bringing attention to different parts of your body. We'd like you to have a go now. Please follow these steps:

● Sit down on a chair and keep your back upright.

● Close your eyes.

● Slowly move your attention to any sensations you might feel in the following parts of your body:

Toes	Ankles	Calves	Hamstrings
Buttocks	Back	Tummy	Chest
Shoulders	Neck	Head	Hands

● As you notice sensations throughout your body, try to notice when your mind has wandered to another topic. When this happens gently re-orient your attention back to the different parts of your body.

October 2023

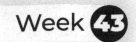 Week **43**

 Summary goal for the week

---

16 **Monday**

---

17 ACT **Tuesday**

---

18 ACT  **Wednesday**

October 2023

19 ACT  Thursday

20 ACT  Friday

21 ACT  Saturday

22 ACT 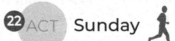 Sunday

"Always remember, your focus determines your reality."

George Lucas

Week 44

Welcome to Week 44.

How did you get on? Did you make progress? Take a moment to reflect on your experience. Were your behaviours this week generally value consistent or value inconsistent?

Record some values and goals that are important to you and which you can try to complete in the next week.

🎯 Goal

🎯 Goal

Exploring Mindfulness Further – Walking Aware

As we mentioned in Week 43, mindfulness exercises are about developing skills that can be generalised to other times and situations when you really need them. One way to encourage generalisation is to practice mindfulness as part of your everyday routine. An interesting way to do this is via a mindful walking exercise, which is something we'd like you to do now. If you are willing then please go for a five-minute walk. Your only job while you walk is to:

1. Notice the things around you.

2. Notice when your mind has wandered away from the things directly in front of you, and bring it back to the present moment.

Walking is an activity that we generally do on automatic pilot. Consequently, as it is so easy for our minds to wander when we walk, we often fail to notice the beauty around us. In fact, when walking mindfully, some people report seeing things for the first time, despite the fact that they had walked the route in question on many occasions! This goes to show that not only is it possible to incorporate mindfulness into our daily routine, but that by doing so we will increase our awareness.

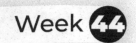

 Summary goal for the week

---

 23 ACT **Monday**

---

 24 ACT **Tuesday**

 **25** ACT **Wednesday**

October 2023

26 ACT  Thursday

27 ACT  Friday

28 ACT  Saturday

29 ACT  Sunday

> *"My father considered a walk among the mountains as the equivalent of churchgoing."*
>
> **Aldous Huxley**

Space for general reflection

Use this space to record the ups and downs of the past few weeks. You may also want to write down what you have learned about yourself and the nature of life.

Space for general reflection

Week 45

Welcome to Week 45.

How did you get on? Did you make progress? Take a moment to reflect on your experience. Were your behaviours this week generally value consistent or value inconsistent?

Record some values and goals that are important to you and which you can try to complete in the next week.

🎯 Goal

🎯 Goal

Exploring the Observing Self – Description and Evaluation

As described in Week 22, we humans so easily build stories about who we think we *'truly'* are and this can be problematic when our stories inhibit what we do. Sometimes a good way of dismantling that way of thinking is to notice the difference between description and evaluation.

For example, suppose I am holding a mobile phone, and I describe it in the following way: *My phone has a black screen, is slightly smaller than my hand and has a camera facility*. Upon seeing my mobile phone you would be able to agree with that sentence from an objective position.

But imagine that I then add the following words to the description: *My phone is the best phone in the world*. At this point you might step in with an objection on the basis that the second sentence isn't a description, it is an evaluation.

We often treat our evaluations as descriptions, which can be unhelpful. For example, we might think of ourselves as not being smart, which is actually closer to an evaluation than a description. In the space below, please complete the *'I am'* sentences with information about you, then circle the statements that are probably evaluation and not fact, because those statements are the ones to watch out for.

I am	I am
I am	I am
I am	I am
I am	I am
I am	I am

Summary goal for the week

 **30   Monday**

---

31   Tuesday

 **1   Wednesday**

2 ACT  **Thursday**

3 ACT  Friday

4 ACT  **Saturday**

5 ACT **Sunday**

> *"Your assumptions are your windows on the world. Scrub them off every once in a while, or the light won't come in."*
>
> **Isaac Asimov**

Week 46

Welcome to Week 46.

How did you get on? Did you make progress? Take a moment to reflect on your experience. Were your behaviours this week generally value consistent or value inconsistent?

_____
_____
_____
_____
_____
_____
_____
_____

Record some values and goals that are important to you and which you can try to complete in the next week.

🎯 Goal

_____
_____
_____

🎯 Goal

_____
_____
_____

Exploring the Observing Self Further – Who is Noticing?

A good way for you to access your observing self, the stable sense of 'I' that exists independently of your thoughts, feelings and stories about yourself, is to engage in a brief mindfulness exercise that requires you to notice who is doing the noticing.

Begin by closing your eyes. Then, for thirty seconds, simply listen to what your mind has to say. The thoughts may be positive or negative, they may be descriptive or evaluative, and they may even stop for a while. Your job for this thirty-second period is simply to watch what happens.

What did you notice? Most people will report mind wandering, as they might do in any typical mindfulness exercise. However, we want you to notice something else. Specifically, we want you to notice that the exercise involved two selves. One 'self', let's call it your *thinking self*, provided you with your thoughts and feelings. Sometimes, it can seem as though we only have a thinking self. But who was watching and listening to the chatter of the thinking self? Who was observing? This is your second sense of self. That is, your *observing self* was there too. Listening, noticing, observing.

 Summary goal for the week

6 **Monday**

7 **Tuesday**

8 **Wednesday**

November 2023

9 ACT  **Thursday**

10 ACT  **Friday**

11 ACT  **Saturday**

12 ACT  **Sunday**

"You have to believe in your heart what you know to be true about yourself. And let that be that."

Mary J Blige

Week 47

Welcome to Week 47.

How did you get on? Did you make progress? Take a moment to reflect on your experience. Were your behaviours this week generally value consistent or value inconsistent?

Exploring Values – Your Heroes

Now that we have further explored the left hand side of the hexaflex, let's look for a final time at your values. One exercise that may be useful at this point involves describing your heroes. In the space below, please name three of your heroes, and detail why they are your heroes.

Some values will pop out of your answers above. That is, some of the qualities that you see in your heroes are probably qualities that you would like to see in yourself. Choose one such value and in the space below record a goal for the coming week that is in line with it.

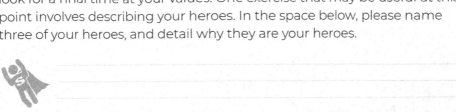 Goal

November 2023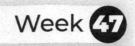

 Summary goal for the week

 **13** Monday

 **14** Tuesday

15 Wednesday

November 2023

16 ACT **Thursday**

17 ACT **Friday**

 **18** ACT **Saturday**

 **19** ACT **Sunday**

---

*"True heroism is not the urge
to surpass all others at whatever cost, but
the urge to serve others at whatever cost."*

Arthur Ashe

Week 48

Welcome to Week 48.

How did you get on? Did you complete the goal related to the heroes exercise? Please take a moment to reflect on your experience. For example, what did you think and/or feel before, during and after you had completed your goal? Also, were your behaviours this week generally value consistent or value inconsistent? Perhaps list notable behaviours in both of those categories?

Please now choose another value from the heroes exercise and in the space below record a bold goal that is in line with it to be completed over the next week.

🎯 Goal

Exploring Committed Action – Waiting for the Wrong Train

The one part of the hexaflex that we haven't yet spoken about explicitly in this diary is committed action. The reason for this is because we have actually asked you to engage in committed action every week by asking you to complete goals. However, now may be the time to think a little bit about it. Why? Because although committed action sounds simple, as you try to act in value consistent ways many unwanted thoughts and feelings may appear. When they do, you will want to continue with your plans for committed action, as the following metaphor illustrates.

Imagine that you are going on a journey to a place that is very special to you (your values). When you get to the train station (the point at which action is required) you see two trains, both of which make the promise of going to your destination. The first train is dirty and uncomfortable. As the second train looks safe and reliable, you decide that it is the better way to travel. However, as you sit on the comfortable train you notice that it never moves. The dirty and uncomfortable train makes many journeys, but your train just doesn't move. Soon you realise that the safe train may never move, and that, in fact, you are sat on the wrong train.

When you attempt to move forward, your mind will try to keep you safe. However, sometimes safety can be akin to being stuck. Sometimes, journeys to a special place may be uncomfortable, but that is not a reason to not make the journey.

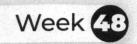

 Summary goal for the week

 20 ACT Monday

21 ACT Tuesday

 22 ACT Wednesday

23 ACT  **Thursday**

24 ACT  **Friday**

25 ACT  **Saturday**

26 ACT **Sunday**

"The most difficult thing is the decision to act, the rest is merely tenacity."

Amelia Earhart

Week 49

Welcome to Week 49.

How did you get on with completing a second goal from the heroes exercise? Please take a moment to reflect on your experience. For example, what did you think and/or feel before, during and after you had completed your goal? Also, were your behaviours this week generally value consistent or value inconsistent? Perhaps list notable behaviours in both of those categories?

In these last few weeks we'd like you to choose some values and goals that seem most important right now. What are the most important changes you'd like to make? Please write a goal or two in the space below to complete in the next week.

 Goal

 Goal

Bringing it all Together: Driving the Bus

Sometimes our minds are just not good for us. They can come up with endless reasons to do or not do different things, and if we pay too much attention to what they say then this can stop us getting on with what we really want to do. Imagine you are about to go to the gym or call a friend, how often has your mind interjected with *'I'm too tired'* or *'I'll do it tomorrow instead'?* It's not that minds are bad or faulty; it's just that they are quick to come up with reasons for not doing things, even when those things matter to us. Starting now (and continuing over the next few weeks), we will describe a popular ACT metaphor that may help you understand the way in which our minds work, and how we often listen to them when we shouldn't.

Imagine that you are a bus driver. You get to drive your bus wherever you like. This is much like your life; you get to move in directions (i.e. values) that are important to you. So here you are, driving your bus of life, and in the distance you see somewhere that you want to go, a place that you would love to get to. For argument's sake, let's call it *lose weight*. Imagine that you start driving towards this place (you are about to go for a run). In the space below please write down some unhelpful thoughts that might pop into your mind.

 Summary goal for the week

 **27** Monday

28 Tuesday

 **29** Wednesday

30 ACT  Thursday

1 ACT  Friday

2 ACT  Saturday

3 ACT Sunday

> "To choose doubt as a
> philosophy of life is akin to choosing
> immobility as a means of transportation."
>
> *Yann Martel*

Space for general reflection

Use this space to record the ups and downs of the past few weeks. You may also want to write down what you have learned about yourself and the nature of life.

Space for general reflection

Week 50

Welcome to Week 50.

How did you get on with your goals? Did you make progress? Take a moment to reflect on your experience. Were your behaviours this week generally value consistent or value inconsistent?

In the space below please record some values and goals that are important to you at this point in your life. Try to complete one or more of them in the next week.

🎯 Goal

🎯 Goal

Bringing it all Together: Passenger Revolt!

So you start driving towards this place that you want to get to and as you do a number of passengers (thoughts) run to the front of the bus and start shouting at you. They can be scary, aggressive, persuasive, sneaky, and are generally unhelpful. They try any way they can to make you drive an alternative route. For example, one passenger might say *'It is too cold to go running now'*.

Imagine that you listened to your passengers and changed your route. What do you think you might feel in the short and the long-term? Please write your thoughts below.

December 2023

 Summary goal for the week

4 **Monday**

5 ACT **Tuesday**

6 **Wednesday**

December 2023

7 ACT Thursday

8 ACT  Friday

9 ACT Saturday   **10** ACT  Sunday

*"We need to start focusing
on what matters — on how we feel,
and how we feel about ourselves."*

Michelle Obama

Week 51

Welcome to Week 51.

How did you get on with your goals? Did you make progress? Take a moment to reflect on your experience. Were your behaviours this week generally value consistent or value inconsistent?

Bringing it all Together: Keep on Driving

So you have listened to your passengers and therefore you are not moving in the direction of what is important to you. A few months go by of driving around when you see the goal again. You start driving towards it. The passengers run to the front of the bus and start being unhelpful. However, this time you keep driving. By doing so, you learn three things:

1. Every time you drive towards that special place the passengers show up. Whenever we start moving towards things that are important to us the mind will probably have something unhelpful to say about it.

2. There is no way to remove the passengers or to make them stop in their sneaky ways. Unwanted thoughts and feelings are like this.

3. Most importantly, as persuasive as these passengers are, they don't have to impact OUR behaviour.

In the space below write down a place that you would like to get to (a goal to complete in the next week), and write down the passengers that you think might be on your bus. What might they look like? Which do you think might be the most powerful in altering your behaviour?

 Goal

Summary goal for the week

 11 Monday

 12 Tuesday

13 Wednesday

December 2023

14 ACT  Thursday

15 ACT Friday

16 ACT  Saturday

17 ACT  Sunday

" *Always turn a negative situation into a positive one.* "

Michael Jordan

Week 52

Welcome to Week 52.

How did you get on? Did you complete a goal related to the passengers on the bus task? Take a moment to reflect on your experience. Were your behaviours this week generally value consistent or value inconsistent?

Record some values and goals that are important to you and which you can try to complete in the next week.

🎯 Goal

🎯 Goal

Ending the Year

That's the end of the year! Congratulations and well done for bringing your values and goals centre stage; we hope that you are living a fuller life as a result of engaging with this diary. And now, let us give you our take home message:

Anything worth doing in life is likely to bring with it a shedload of discomfort. As a good rule of thumb, the more something matters, the more challenge, uncertainty and angst we will feel. Many people respond to these things by staying in their comfort zone. However, you don't have to. You can move out of that comfort zone and learn for yourself that that's where the magic of life happens.

How do we do this? First, we need to decide what we really want to do and how we want to do it. If you know this already then great, but if you're unsure then a good place to start is by reviewing your values and writing some goals related to them. Set yourself some short-term targets and some that are harder or more challenging.

Whatever your goals, try to move yourself out of your comfort zone – but expect a host of unwanted thoughts and feelings to pop up on the way. When they come along remember to embrace them willingly, defuse unhelpful thoughts, maintain contact with the present moment and hold your self-stories lightly.

We hope you've found our year together useful, and we wish you the best of luck going forward.

Nic and Freddy

Where the magic happens...

Your Comfort Zone

Summary goal for the week

---

18 **Monday**

---

19 **Tuesday**

---

20  **Wednesday**

21 ACT  Thursday

22 ACT  Friday

23 ACT  Saturday

24 ACT Sunday

"You can't just sit and wait for people to give you that golden dream. You've got to make it happen."

Diana Ross

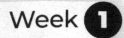
 Summary goal for the week

 **25** **Monday**

 **26** **Tuesday**

 **27** **Wednesday**

28 ACT  Thursday

29 ACT Friday

30 ACT  Saturday

31 ACT Sunday

> *"It always seems impossible until it's done."*
>
> *Nelson Mandela*

Space for general reflection

Use this space to record the ups and downs of the past few weeks. You may also want to write down what you have learned about yourself and the nature of life.

Space for general reflection

Goal Bank

 Goal

 Goal

 Goal

 Goal

 Goal

Goal Bank

🎯 Goal

🎯 Goal

🎯 Goal

🎯 Goal

🎯 Goal

Goal Bank

 Goal

 Goal

 Goal

 Goal

 Goal

Goal Bank

 Goal

 Goal

 Goal

 Goal

 Goal

About Nic and Freddy

Dr Nic Hooper

Nic is an expert in clinical psychology and a Lecturer in Psychology at Cardiff University. He has authored many scientific articles, book chapters and books including *The Research Journey of Acceptance and Commitment Therapy* and *The Unbreakable Student*. Nic is a co-director of Connect (which is an organisation that offers a psychological wellbeing curriculum for primary school children) and for two years he sat on the board of the Association for Contextual Behavioral Science (ACBS), the 8,000-member organization that oversees a lot of ACT related work. He is the co-author of *The Acceptance and Commitment Therapy (ACT) Journal*.

Dr Freddy Jackson Brown

Freddy is an HCPC (Health and Care Professions Council) registered chartered clinical psychologist with 20 years' experience working with children and families in the NHS. His practice is child centred and focuses on helping individuals learn the communication and everyday living skills needed to live a more independent and fulfilling life. He has published a range of peer reviewed articles, book chapters and books including *When Young People with Intellectual Disabilities and Autism Hit Puberty* and *ACT for Dummies*. His interests include child development, language and communication, challenging behaviour, staff systems, emotional literacy and supervision. He is the co-author of *The Acceptance and Commitment Therapy (ACT) Journal*.